ANCIENT EGYPT

JANE SHUTER

Heinemann

www.heinemann.co.uk/library
Visit our website to find out more information about **Heinemann Library** books.

To order:
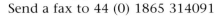
☎ Phone 44 (0) 1865 888066
🗎 Send a fax to 44 (0) 1865 314091
💻 Visit the Heinemann Bookshop at www.heinemann.co.uk/library to browse our catalogue and order online.

First published in Great Britain by Heinemann Library, Halley Court, Jordan Hill, Oxford OX2 8EJ, part of Harcourt Education. Heinemann is a registered trademark of Harcourt Education Ltd.

© Harcourt Education Ltd 2006
First published in paperback in 2006.
The moral right of the proprietor has been asserted.

Editorial: Jilly, Attwood, Kathy Peltan and Vicki Yates
Design: David Poole and Tokay Interactive Ltd
Picture Research: Hannah Taylor
Production: Camilla Smith

Originated by Chroma Graphics (Overseas) Pte. Ltd
Printed in China by WKT Company Limited

ISBN 0 431 07902 1 (hardback)
10 09 08 07 06
10 9 8 7 6 5 4 3 2 1

ISBN 0 431 07908 0 (paperback)
10 09 08 07 06
10 9 8 7 6 5 4 3 2 1

British Library Cataloguing in Publication Data
Shuter, Jane
Ancient Egypt
932'.01
A full catalogue record for this book is available from the British Library.

Acknowledgements
The publishers would like to thank the following for permission to reproduce photographs: Ancient Art & Architecture Collection pp. **24**, **26** (Ronald Sheridan); Ashmolean Museum p. **12**; Corbis pp. **7** (Sandro Vannini), **10** (Yann Arthus-Bertrand), **11** (Gianni Dagli Orti), **14** (Charles and Josette Lenars), **19b** (Michael Nicholson), p. **28** (Carmen Redondo), **29l** (Archivo Iconografico S.A.); Harcourt Education Ltd pp. **4** (Peter Evans), **9**, **13**, **15**, **18**, **22**, **27** (Phil Cooke and Magnet Harlequin); Trustees of the British Museum pp. **16**, **20**; Werner Forman Archive pp. **17**, **25** (British Museum), **21** (Egyptian Museum, Cairo) pp. **19t**, **23**; Dr Caroline Wilkinson, University of Manchester p **29r**.

Cover photograph of the Colossi of Rameses II and Nafertari, reproduced with permission of Corbis Royalty Free.

The publishers would like to thank Robyn Hardyman, Bob Rees and Caroline Landon for their assistance in the preparation of this book.

Every effort has been made to contact copyright holders of any material reproduced in this book. Any omissions will be rectified in subsequent printings if notice is given to the publishers.

Any words appearing in the text in bold, **like this**, are explained in the glossary.

Contents

Exploring further

Throughout the book you will find links to the Heinemann Explore CD-ROM and website at www.heinemannexplore.co.uk. Follow the links to discover more about a topic.

What do the symbols mean?

The following symbols are used throughout the book:

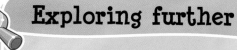 Source

 See for yourself

 Biography

What do we already know about ancient Egypt?

Where was it?

Ancient Egypt was in north east Africa, roughly where modern Egypt is today. The River Nile ran the whole length of the country. The ancient Egyptians grew their crops on the banks of the Nile. The land further away from the river was **desert**.

The Egyptians built pyramids as tombs for their pharaohs. The Great Pyramid at Giza was built in about 2660 BC for the pharaoh Khufu, also known as Cheops. It stands 162 metres (531 feet) high, and is made of **sandstone**. It was once coated with gleaming white **limestone** and the top capped with shining gold.

When was it?

The ancient Egyptian civilization lasted from about 3100 BC to 30 BC. It is usually divided into three main parts. Historians call these the Old Kingdom, the Middle Kingdom, and the New Kingdom.

The Old Kingdom

The Old Kingdom lasted from 2686 BC to 2181 BC. The great stone **pyramids** at Giza were built at this time. At the end of the Old Kingdom, there were some difficult years because Egypt did not have a strong ruler.

The Middle Kingdom

The Middle Kingdom lasted from 2055 BC to 1650 BC. It started when a strong **pharaoh** took control and more pyramids were built. There was a lot of trade with nearby countries. At the end of the Middle Kingdom, there was another difficult time. Foreign rulers, called the Hyksos, took over part of Egypt.

The New Kingdom

The New Kingdom lasted from 1550 BC to 1069 BC. Egypt was strong again. Pharaohs and other important people were buried in tombs cut into the rock in the **Valley of the Kings**. The pharaoh Tutankhamun ruled during the New Kingdom.

The Late Period was from 747 BC to 332 BC. During this time the Nubian people took over Egypt. The Nubians were followed by the Assyrian people, then the Persians, and then the Greeks. Finally, Egypt became part of the Roman **Empire** in 30 BC.

How do we know?

We can learn about ancient Egypt by looking at objects found in the tombs. The Egyptians buried people with lots of possessions, and decorated the tomb walls with paintings and writings.

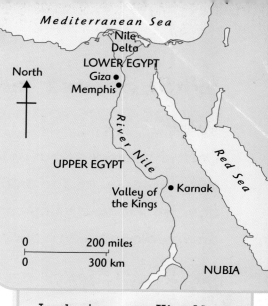

In about 3100 BC, King Menes united Upper and Lower Egypt, and built a new capital city at Memphis.

3100 BC — Upper and Lower Egypt united 3100 BC

2650 BC first pyramid built

Early Period 3100–2686 BC

Old Kingdom 2686–2181 BC

Middle Kingdom 2055–1650 BC

New Kingdom 1550–1069 BC

Late Period 747–332 BC

332–30 BC Greeks take over Egypt

1 BC — 30 BC Romans take over Egypt

Exploring further

The **Heinemann Explore** website and CD-ROM include text on all the key topics about ancient Egypt. You will also find pictures, biographies, written sources, and lots of activities to explore. Start at the Contents screen. Click on the blue words in the list and off you go!

What can we learn about ancient Egypt from one object?

Different objects tell us different things about ancient Egypt. The more things we look at, the more we find out. Look at as many objects as you can. However, you can find out a lot even from one object. Here are some questions to ask about the object you are looking at:

Who made it?

- Was it made by a person with special skills or could anyone have made it?
- Was it made by more than one person, like the **pyramids**? If so, was it made by people who had various different skills?

What was it made from?

- Was it made from an expensive material, like gold?
- Was it made from a cheap material, like wood?

What was it for?

- Was it made as a useful thing, like a wooden farming tool or a boat?
- Was it made as an ornament, like a necklace or earrings?
- Was it made to last, like the pyramids?

Sometimes, objects are made for more than one reason. A beautiful glass jar for make-up is a useful thing, but it is also an ornament because it has been made to look nice. On the next page we are going to see what we can learn from Tutankhamun's **mummy**.

Tutankhamun's mummy was placed inside a coffin made of solid gold that weighs 110 kilograms (242 pounds). The gold mask shows the young king's face. From this we learn that:

- the ancient Egyptians thought highly of their pharaohs
- some ancient Egyptians were very skilled craftsmen
- they had gold and precious stones, which they either bought from abroad or had in Egypt
- they took time to bury people carefully
- they made death masks that looked like the dead person.

Tutankhamun

Tutankhamun became **pharaoh** in 1336 BC. He was only nine years old, so he was too young to rule Egypt himself. Instead, the country was run by his two most powerful advisors, Ay and Horemheb. Tutankhamun married a royal princess, Ankhesenamun. We do not know much more about his life. Tutankhamun died suddenly, aged eighteen, in 1327 BC. His tomb was still full of treasure when **archaeologists** found it, over 3000 years later. From looking at his mummy, historians think he might have died from a blow to the head. Some historians think that Ay might have wanted to kill Tutankhamun, so that he could become pharaoh himself. We do know that Ay became the next pharaoh. He also married Tutankhamun's **widow**, Ankhesenamun.

Exploring further

Use the Heinemann Explore CD-ROM or visit the website to find out more about:

- the discovery of Tutankhamun's tomb by Howard Carter in 1922. Look in 'Exploring, Key People and Events'.

- a video showing wall paintings inside a tomb. Look in 'Media Bank, Beliefs'.

What does the landscape tell us about life in ancient Egypt?

Most people's lives are shaped by the landscape and weather of the place where they live. The lives of the ancient Egyptians certainly were. Egypt is hot and dry all year round and it hardly ever rains. Most of the land is **desert**.

The River Nile

The most important landscape feature in ancient Egypt was the River Nile. It ran the whole length of the country. People lived along the banks of the river where they could grow crops. They could not move far from the water because the rest of the land was desert. People also used the river for transport, both for themselves and for goods.

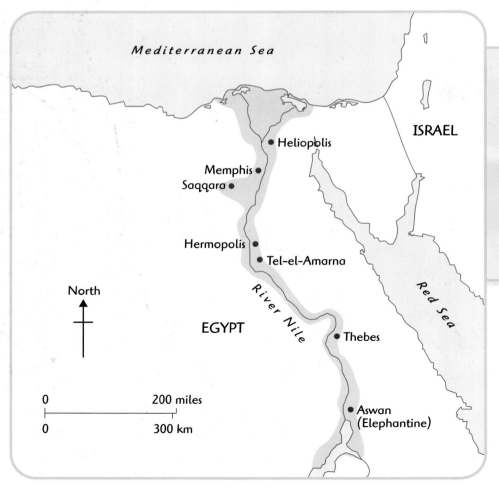

Every year the darker area shown here was flooded by the Nile, and could be used for farming. The map also shows that cities, shown by red dots, developed along the Nile.

Natural defences

You can see from the map that ancient Egypt had natural borders that cut it off from its neighbours. It had desert to the east and west, the Mediterranean Sea and the Nile **delta** to the north. There was also a huge waterfall in the Nile at Elephantine (now Aswan), to the south. These natural defences made Egypt hard to attack.

A useful desert

Although food could not be grown in the desert, it too had its uses. The ancient Egyptians found gold and precious stones in the rocks under the sand. These made Egypt rich. They also used the desert for burials. The hot, dry sand was suitable for **preserving** remains.

Exploring further

Use the Heinemann Explore CD-ROM or website to find out more about trade with foreign lands for goods such as copper, ivory, ebony, and ostrich feathers. Look in 'Digging Deeper, Ancient Egypt, Trade and tribute'.

The land away from the area flooded by the Nile was desert, and so impossible to farm. Even today this is true.

How much of the life of ancient Egypt depended on the River Nile?

Without the River Nile, the civilization of ancient Egypt would never have existed. It does not rain much in Egypt, and without the annual flooding of the Nile, the land would be a **desert**. There would be nowhere to grow food to eat.

Floods and food

Every year, on almost exactly the same date, 15 July, the river began to rise. By October it spread gently over the flat land on either side. When the water went down, thick mud was left behind. This mud was the only place in Egypt where crops would grow. To avoid the floods, people had to build their houses on high ground.

This is part of a song, written in about 2020 BC, which shows how important the flooding was to the ancient Egyptians.

Lord of the fish, he sends the birds flying south as he rises,
He is father to the barley and the wheat.
If he is slow to rise, people hold their breath.
They grow fierce as food runs short and many starve.
When the flooding is absent, greed stalks the land,
Rich and poor alike wander the roads, homeless.
Yet when the river rises, sparkling, the land rejoices,
Every stomach will be filled.

Crops are still grown today on the area of land made **fertile** by the Nile floods.

Contact with other countries

The ancient Egyptians could usually grow enough food and make everything they needed. However, there were some years when the Nile did not flood much. Less mud was left when the floods went down. Farmers could not grow as much food, so they had to trade with other countries to get **grain**.

Transport

As well as providing the soil for growing food, the Nile and its canals provided the main means of transport. The river was always full of boats of many sizes. They carried families visiting friends, traders sailing between riverside towns or into the Mediterranean, and builders moving the great stone blocks and statues from the quarries to new tomb and temple sites.

Precious stones and materials to make treasures were transported down the Nile. This brooch belonged to King Tutankhamun. You can read more about King Tutankhamun on page 7.

Exploring further

Use the Heinemann Explore CD-ROM or website to find out more about the importance of the Nile. Try the Activity 'The Nile'.

What do objects that have survived tell us about the ancient Egyptians?

Most of the objects that have survived from ancient Egyptian times are to do with burials. They include **pyramids**, tombs, and all the things that were buried with dead people. These objects tell us what the Egyptians thought about death. But they also tell us about how they lived their lives.

Objects for the afterlife

The Egyptians believed that people needed many things in the **afterlife**. People were buried with clothes, jewellery, furniture, and tools. Models of boats and houses have also been found. Some people were even buried with food and drink!

All these buried objects tell us a lot about everyday life in ancient Egypt. They tell us what people ate and drank, and what clothes they wore. They tell us what they had in their houses, and what jobs they did.

Some things, like boats, were too big to fit into the tomb, so small models like this one were made. We can tell what size the real boat would have been from the size of the model people.

Towns and villages

Remains of a few towns and villages have also survived from ancient Egypt. From these we can learn about the homes of ordinary people, and their daily lives.

Hekanakhte

Hekanakhte was a **scribe** and **priest**, who lived and worked in Thebes in about 2000 BC. He was not an important official, and normally we would not have known anything about him. Luckily, a set of letters has survived that he wrote to his family while he was away on business. They give us a rare look at an ordinary Egyptian family.

This wall painting is from the **Valley of the Kings**. It shows a scribe weighing and recording gold and silver.

These are the people in Hekanakhte's family:

- Hekanakhte
- Iutenheb, his second wife
- Merisu, the oldest son, an adult, who is in charge while Hekanakhte is away
- Sahathor, the next oldest son, an adult, who is with his father, but carrying letters to and fro
- Sanebniut, the third son
- Inpu, the fourth son, who is still a boy
- Snefru, the youngest son, who is spoiled by everyone
- Ipi, Hekanakhte's mother
- At least two daughters called Hotepet and Nefret.

Exploring further

Use the Heinemann Explore CD-ROM or website to find out more about:

- the work of scribes. Look in 'Digging Deeper, Ancient Egypt, Education'.

- learning to be a scribe, from an original document. Look in 'Written Sources'.

The family also had a maid called Senen and various other servants. The letters tell us that the children of Hekanakhte's first wife do not like his new wife. Hekanakhte tells them that they should treat her better. He also tells his family how they should be farming his land.

What do objects that have survived tell us about farming in ancient Egypt?

Paintings of farming scenes have been found on the walls of tombs. Some examples of crops have even survived, dried in the **desert** sand.

Growing crops

The farming year was controlled by the flooding of the Nile. In July, the river began to rise and flood the fields beside it. It left behind a thick layer of mud that made the land very **fertile**. In late October, the flood waters started to go down. The farmers then started work, ploughing the ground and planting seeds.

Farmers had to grow crops for food. They always planted **grain** first because it was the most important food. They used it to make bread, porridge, and beer.

The farmers watered the grain for many weeks to make the seeds grow into plants. At **harvest** time they cut down the plants. Then they planted a second crop, usually beans or another vegetable.

While the River Nile was flooding, farmers could not grow crops because their land was underwater. Instead, they mended their tools and looked after their animals. For some days every year, they had to do building work for the **pharaoh**.

This painting shows farmers harvesting crops. You can see that farmers had only simple wooden tools to work with. They needed to be mended, and replaced quite often.

This model shows animals that were farmed in ancient Egypt. It was made to go in a tomb to provide the dead person with farming equipment and animals for the **afterlife**.

Saving water

During the flood, there was too much water. But when the flood went down, the water disappeared. To save water, farmers trapped the flood water in big ponds. They dug ditches leading from the ponds all around their fields. The ditches carried water to where the crops were growing. This way of saving and using water is called **irrigation**.

Keeping animals

Ancient Egyptian farmers kept animals. They got meat and milk from cows, sheep, and goats. They used their skins too for clothes and sandals. They kept ducks and geese for their eggs and meat, and bees for their honey.

 Pictures of farming scenes on tomb walls often have **hieroglyphs** of farmers talking with each other. Here are two of them.

'A fine, cool day! The oxen are pulling the plough. The weather is good, let us work for the master.'

'Go on, guide it! Hurry, hurry you in front! Drive the oxen! Mind your feet. Watch out, the master's here and he's watching us!'

'Hey! You're pulling the flax up by the roots, not picking it and on such a good day for work!'

'You make sure you are doing your work properly before you criticize me!'

 # Hapi

Hapi was the god who controlled the River Nile. Ancient Egyptians prayed to him for a good flood. A low flood could mean no food for many of the poorest people. A high flood was bad too – homes would be flooded. A low flood was feared the most.

What do objects that have survived tell us about food in ancient Egypt?

Bread and beer were the most important foods in ancient Egypt. We know that they were important because they were featured in many tomb objects and paintings.

Bread

There were many types of bread made with flour from different **grains**. The flour was made by crushing the grain and shaking off the outsides. The grain was then ground between two stones. The flour had bits of stone in it, which came from the grinding. So the bread was gritty and wore away the Egyptians' teeth! The flour was mixed with water and baked in ovens.

This model showing how bread was made was found in the tomb of a **pharaoh**. The grain is ground, then the flour is sieved. It is then made into dough and shaped into loaves.

Beer

Beer was made from partly-baked barley bread, barley, and water. This was all mashed up together, left for a few days, and then strained into beer jars. It was still thick and lumpy and had to be drunk through a wooden strainer (like a thick straw).

Cooking

People did not cook inside their homes. Ordinary people had a bread oven in their yard. They cooked most other foods on open fires in the yard or on the roof. They ate their main meal outside inside the evening, when it was cooler.

Animals

Cows, sheep, and goats were kept for milk and meat. Ducks and geese were kept for eggs and meat. Fish were often kept in the duck ponds. Bees were kept in hives for honey to sweeten food and drink.

The Egyptians also hunted wild animals and birds, and caught fish to eat. Tomb paintings show the river and marshes full of birds and fish.

This tomb painting shows a man fishing in the marshes. Fishermen made a living catching fish. Some people made a living hunting wild birds for rich people to eat. Rich people went hunting for fun, when they felt like it.

 This comes from an ancient Egyptian story written in about 2000 BC, called *The Tale of Sinuhe*. It shows what the ancient Egyptians thought of as luxury.

I became ruler of that beautiful place. Each day people brought me food. I drank wine every day. I ate cooked meat, or roast duck, or dishes of wild animals. They hunted for me and they fished for me, adding to the animals I caught when hunting with my greyhounds. They fed me sweet things too, milk and many baked things.

Vegetables

The ancient Egyptians also ate a lot of vegetables, including beans, onions, leeks, garlic, and cucumbers. They ate fruit too, such as grapes, figs, and dates. Only rich people ate a lot of meat and fish.

 ## Exploring further

Use the Heinemann Explore CD-ROM or website to find out more about:

- a picture of an Egyptian using a strainer to drink beer. Look in 'Pictures, Everyday Life'.

- how Egyptian doctors used vegetables and herbs as medicines. Look in 'Digging Deeper, Farming and food'.

What do buildings that have survived tell us about ancient Egypt?

Homes

Ancient Egyptian towns were built close to the river, on high ground. All ancient Egyptians lived in houses made from mud bricks. The mud bricks have long since crumbled away, but some stone bases of the houses have survived. Houses had thick walls and small windows to keep out the heat. People worked, cooked, and ate on the flat roof. Even rich people did not have much furniture. Ordinary people sat on mats on the ground.

Temples

Temples were built of stone, so many have survived. The walls were painted white, then decorated with pictures and **hieroglyphs**. Some of these paintings have survived.

Temples were homes for the gods. Ordinary people were not usually allowed into them. A large temple would have its own farmland. It might have a library joined on to it, and a school for rich boys. There would also be houses for farmers and craftsmen.

The temple buildings had a high wall all around them. Inside, there were rooms and courtyards. The most important room was the **shrine**. Only the most important **priest**, called the High Priest, could go into the shrine. Inside the shrine was a statue of the god or goddess. The High Priest looked after the statue. He prayed to it, washed it, and offered it food.

Only the stone bases of the ancient Egyptian village at Deir el-Medina remain. The craftsmen who worked on the tombs in the **Valley of the Kings** lived here. The houses were packed tightly together in terraces without gardens.

Temples were painted in bright colours. Where they have been buried under sand, the colours have been protected from the sun and wind. These huge pillars are from the temple at Karnak. They are decorated with carvings.

Tombs

During the New Kingdom period, all **pharaohs** were buried in the Valley of the Kings, near Thebes. They were buried in tombs cut deep into the rock. The tombs had many rooms, linked by tunnels. The walls of these rooms were decorated with paintings and carvings. The coffin was in one room, the pharaoh's treasure was in another.

See for yourself

Cleopatra's Needle

Cleopatra's Needle is an enormous stone **obelisk**. It stands beside the River Thames in London. The obelisk was made for pharaoh Tuthmose III, and is carved with **hieroglyphics** praising him. It was first put up in Egypt in about 1500 BC. Extra inscriptions were added about 200 years later by Rameses II, to commemorate his great victories in battle.

It is known as Cleopatra's Needle because it was brought to London from Alexandria, the royal city of Cleopatra in Egypt. For centuries it had lain neglected in the sand. Then in 1819, it was given to Britain. It was brought to London and placed on the Thames Embankment in 1878.

What do writing and art that have survived tell us about ancient Egypt?

Writing

The ancient Egyptians developed writing by about 3100 BC. People who could read and write were called **scribes**. They used brushes and ink to write on rolls of paper called **papyrus**.

In the first kind of writing, people just drew a picture of what they wanted to say, so a picture of a mat meant 'a mat'. Later, a more complicated kind of writing was used, called **hieroglyphics**. In hieroglyphic writing, the pictures began to mean sounds too. One word could be made up of several pictures.

Hieroglyphics were a very slow way of writing. They were used for important things, such as decorating tombs. There was a much simpler and quicker kind of writing, called **hieratic** writing. This was used for ordinary letters and lists.

This is a page of papyrus from *The Book of the Dead*. It has both hieroglyphic writing and a painting. The painting shows the funeral of a man called Ani. The writing below is a spell to help Ani in the **afterlife**.

Art

Ancient Egyptian art has lots of detail, and the colours are still bright after thousands of years. Artists painted on walls and on papyrus. There are paintings of people, gods, and everyday life. Tomb models show everyday activities such as farming and cooking.

Artists

The names of the artists whose works filled the tombs, temples, and palaces of ancient Egypt are almost all lost because they did not sign their work. We know one artist's name by accident – in one tomb scene he painted himself decorating a statue. An admirer later copied the painting and added his name: Houy.

Jewellery

Everyone loved jewellery and wore as much as they could afford. Favourite stones were blue lapis lazuli, red carnelian and greenish-blue turquoise. Gold was mined in the desert. All gold was sent to the **pharaoh's** workshops because it all belonged to him.

This bracelet is from the tomb of the governor Amenemope. It is decorated with blue lapis lazuli creatures. The patterns are made from red carnelian, turquoise, and other precious stones.

Exploring further

Use the Heinemann Explore CD-ROM or website to find out more about:

* hieratic writing. Look in 'Exploring, Everyday Life, Writing'.

* ancient Egyptian artists and craftsmen, their materials and methods. Look in 'Digging Deeper, Ancient Egyptian art'.

What does technology that has survived tell us about ancient Egypt?

Irrigation

There was not much water in ancient Egypt. It hardly ever rained there. Most water came from the River Nile. The ancient Egyptians invented clever ways of getting water from the Nile to their fields. When the Nile flooded, they trapped the water in ponds around their fields. The water was let out into ditches in the fields when it was needed. This way of saving and using water is called **irrigation**. Irrigation is still important in Egypt today.

Herodotus was a Greek historian. He visited Egypt in 450 BC. This is taken from his writings.

*When the Nile overflows, the whole country becomes a sea, only the towns are above water. At these times water transport is used all over the country, and you can sail right up to the **pyramids** … All Egypt is flat, but they do not use horses or wheeled traffic. This is because of the huge numbers of ditches that cut the country up. These ditches bring water to inland towns, which before had to rely on stale well water.*

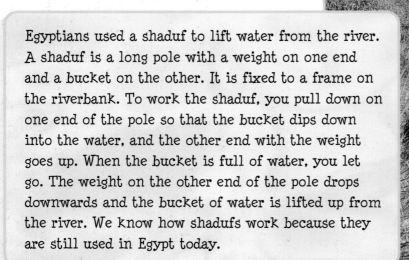

Egyptians used a shaduf to lift water from the river. A shaduf is a long pole with a weight on one end and a bucket on the other. It is fixed to a frame on the riverbank. To work the shaduf, you pull down on one end of the pole so that the bucket dips down into the water, and the other end with the weight goes up. When the bucket is full of water, you let go. The weight on the other end of the pole drops downwards and the bucket of water is lifted up from the river. We know how shadufs work because they are still used in Egypt today.

Maps

The Egyptians were the first people to make detailed maps of places, and of the stars in the sky. Most sky maps were made by priests, to work out when to hold religious ceremonies. The priests worked out the difference between the stars and the planets. They knew about five of the planets: Mars, Saturn, Jupiter, Venus, and Mercury.

Imhotep

Imhotep is best known as an **architect**. He designed the very first pyramid. This pyramid was made of stone and had stepped sides. It was built as a tomb for Djoser at a place called Saqqara. Later pyramids followed the same pattern. We think that Imhotep was the first person who used stone for building. Before his pyramid, all buildings in ancient Egypt were made from mud bricks.

Imhotep was also a **scribe** and a **priest**. He was an important official and doctor for the **pharaoh** Djoser. Imhotep collected lots of **papyrus** scrolls. These contained useful information that could be passed on to other people. Imhotep was buried close to the pharaoh Djoser. This was a great honour for a person who was not one of the royal family. Hundreds of years after his death, Egyptians began to worship him as a god of learning and medicine.

There are pictures of ancient Egyptian tools and technology on tomb walls. This is a wood carving that shows another official of pharaoh Djoser. He was the Chief of Dentists and Physicians. He is carrying the tools of a scribe, and around him are a doctor's surgical instruments.

Exploring further

Use the Heinemann Explore CD-ROM or website to find out more about other ancient Egyptian inventions, such as locks and lighthouses. Look in 'Digging Deeper, Discoveries and inventions'.

23

What did the ancient Egyptians believe about life after death?

The ancient Egyptians believed that people came back to life after they died. They believed that dead people were judged by the gods and goddesses, and then lived in a place called the Field of Reeds. Here, everything was like real life, only perfect. This new life was called the **afterlife**.

A body to live in

The body of a dead person had to be kept whole. This was so that they could live again in the afterlife. The ancient Egyptians found a way of stopping bodies from rotting away, called **embalming**.

Plenty of possessions

Dead people needed lots of things for a comfortable afterlife. They were buried with food, drink, furniture, clothes, and jewellery.

This page of **papyrus** shows the funeral of a man called Hunefer. He lived in about 1310 BC, and was a very important official working for the **pharaoh** Sety I. In the picture, Hunefer's wife and daughter mourn, while three priests perform a ritual called 'The Opening of the Mouth'. This was believed to give the dead person back their power of speech, and allow them to eat and drink. The white building on the far right is the tomb.

Caring for the dead

Children had to bury their parents properly. They prayed for them for a long time after they had died. They took food and drink to the chapels near their burial places. It was thought very important to be cared for after death. This is why having children was so important.

This is a letter carved by a man on the back of a memorial stone for his dead wife. It was written in about 2050 BC.

How are you? Are you happy in the afterlife? Look! I am your beloved on earth, so fight for me, speak for me. I have made sure you were buried properly so drive off the illness in my limbs!

This model found in a tomb is of a servant girl. She carries bread and meat as an offering for the person buried in the tomb. Other model figures were also buried in tombs. These were workers, to do duty work for the dead person in the afterlife, such as working on the pyramids for the pharaoh. The models were called shabtis.

Mummies

To stop bodies rotting away, and to keep them whole, they were **embalmed**. First, the embalmers took out all the soft inside parts of the body, such as the brain and the stomach. Then they washed out the inside of the body with a salty liquid. They left the body soaking in a kind of salt for 70 days, to dry it out. They then cleaned the body, dried it, and wrapped it in long strips of cloth that had been soaked in oil. Bodies that have been embalmed are called **mummies**.

Next, the mummy was put into a **coffin** made in the shape of a person. The coffin was given to the **priests** to bury the body.

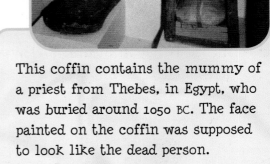

This coffin contains the mummy of a priest from Thebes, in Egypt, who was buried around 1050 BC. The face painted on the coffin was supposed to look like the dead person.

How do we know?

Scientists today can use modern technology to see inside mummies without unwrapping them. They can also take tiny pieces from an unwrapped mummy and learn about the age and sex of the person, and even what diseases they had.

Tombs

The more important a person was, the more complicated their tomb was. In later times, **pharaohs** were no longer buried in **pyramids**. Instead, they were buried in **tombs** cut into the rock at a place called the **Valley of the Kings**, near the city of Thebes. These tombs had lots of tunnels leading to different rooms. The coffin of the **pharaoh** was placed in one room. His treasure and his family's coffins were put in the other rooms. Other important people were also buried in tombs like this.

Tomb decoration

The walls of tombs were decorated with paintings and carvings. We can learn a lot about the lives of the ancient Egyptians from looking at them.

Finding tombs

Over the centuries, tomb robbers found many ancient Egyptian tombs and took away their treasures. In the early 1900s, **archaeologists** were searching in the Valley of the Kings for undiscovered tombs. One of them was an Englishman called Howard Carter. In 1922, he found the tomb of the pharaoh Tutankhamun. It was full of treasure, everything the pharaoh would need in the **afterlife**.

This was the tomb of pharaoh Rameses VI. It was discovered and robbed more than 3000 years ago. The robbers broke open the coffin to get at the mummy, which would have been covered in gold. The wall paintings are still clearly visible.

This is part of Howard Carter's account of the discovery of Tutankhamun's tomb. It was written soon after the treasure was found.

Slowly, desperately slowly, the door was cleared. I made a small hole in the top left-hand corner. Widening the hole a little, I put the candle through the gap and peered in … At first I could see nothing. My eyes got used to the light. As they did, things slowly took shape. I could see strange animals, statues, and gold – everywhere the glint of gold. I was too amazed to speak. Lord Carnarvon, unable to wait any longer, asked, 'Can you see anything?' It was all I could do to say, 'Yes, wonderful things.'

Exploring further

Use the Heinemann Explore CD-ROM or visit the website to find out more about:

- the tombs in the Valley of the Kings. Look in 'Digging Deeper, Valley of the Kings'.

- the story of Howard Carter's discovery of Tutankhamun. Look in 'Exploring, Key People and Events'.

What can we learn about ancient Egypt from what has survived?

By studying the places and objects that have survived, we can learn a lot about the ancient Egyptians, their way of life and beliefs. The dry **desert** sand has preserved bodies, tombs and other objects that would have rotted away in wetter places.

Tombs

Most of the objects we have from ancient Egypt have been found in tombs by **archaeologists**. Historians have translated writings, both on **papyrus** and carved in stone, that were found in the tombs and in the great temples built by the **pharaohs**. Ruins have also been uncovered of the village, Deir-el-Medina, where the workers who built the tombs once lived.

On the west bank of the Nile, a rocky, desert valley was chosen as the burial place of the pharaohs. This is the Valley of the Kings. The tombs there tell a story more than 3000 years old. On the walls of the tombs are pictures and writings that tell of the pharaohs buried inside them, and the civilization they ruled over.

This is from a hymn to the god Amun. It might have been written by pharaoh Akhenaten in about 1350 BC.

You place each person in his proper place in life
And you make sure he needs nothing.
Each has enough food
And the amount of life that is right for him.

See for yourself

The British Museum, London

The British Museum has the biggest and best collection of objects from ancient Egypt to be found anywhere outside modern Egypt. It includes massive carved stone heads, paintings, carved coffins, painted coffins, and mummies.

The Rosetta Stone is carved with **hieroglyphic** and **demotic** writing, and some Greek writing. It was found in Egypt in 1799. Using the Greek as a guide, a historian worked out what the hieroglyphics on the stone meant. That has made it possible for historians to work out the meaning of other Egyptian hieroglyphics, and so learn more about the ancient Egyptian way of life.

X-rays and new scanning methods were used to look inside the mummy of an Egyptian priest called Nesperennub. Scientists then made this model of his face. You can find out more and see his skeleton in the British Museum's *Mummy: The Inside Story* display.

Timeline

BC

3100–2686	The Early Period
c.3100	Upper and Lower Egypt are united under one ruler. A new capital city is built at Memphis. **Hieroglyphics** are developed as a written language.
2686–2181	The Old Kingdom
2667–2648	Djoser is **pharaoh**, Imhotep is his official
2500–2181	The major period in which **pyramids** are built
2660	The Great Pyramid for pharaoh Khufu is built
2650	The step pyramid for pharaoh Djoser is built
2181–2055	The First Intermediate Period, when Egypt is divided. No pyramids are built.
2055–1650	The Middle Kingdom. Pyramid building begins again.
2000	Hekanakhte is living and writing
1550–1069	The New Kingdom. Pharaohs and royal families are buried in rock-cut tombs in the **Valley of the Kings** and Valley of the Queens. The workmen's village of Deir el-Medina is built near by. The first evidence of the use of a **shaduf** to lift water from the River Nile.
1352–1336	Akhenaten rules, and builds a new capital city at el-Armana
1336–1327	Tutankhamun rules
1184–1153	Rameses III rules
1150	The first known map is drawn, of gold mines at Wadi Hammamat
747–332	The Late Period. Egypt is controlled by Libyans, followed by Nubians, Assyrians, and then Persians.
270	The first ever lighthouse is built at Alexandria
51–30	Cleopatra rules
30	The Romans take over Egypt

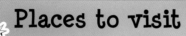

Places to visit

British Museum, London
The magnificent collection of ancient Egyptian artefacts includes colossal sculptures, mummies, and works of art found inside tombs.

The Manchester Museum, Manchester
Home to one of the largest collections of ancient Egyptian artefacts in the United Kingdom. the collection includes a large section on ancient Egyptian mummies.

Petrie Museum of Egyptian Archaeology, London
The collection is based on the life and work of archaeologist and Egyptologist William Flinders Petrie. It includes many objects related to life and death in ancient Egypt.

Ashmolean Museum, Oxford
The museum has a good collection of wall paintings, mummies, and other ancient Egyptian objects.

Royal Museum, Edinburgh
The museum's collection of objects from ancient Egypt includes mummy masks, canopic jars, and statues.

Glossary

afterlife ancient Egyptians believed that the dead came back to life in the afterlife. Their afterlife was in a place called the Field of Reeds, which was just like real life, but perfect.

archaeologist person who looks for, digs up, and studies things left from past times

architect person who designs buildings

delta marshy land of Lower Egypt. The Nile splits into twelve main channels before it flows into the sea.

demotic shorthand version of hieroglyphic writing

desert dry place that has little or no rainfall all year round

embalm stopping a body from rotting, usually by drying it out and wrapping it in strips of cloth

empire a country and all the parts of other lands that it also rules

fertile soil that is good for growing crops

grain fat seeds that can be eaten. Barley wheat, rye, oats, and rice are all grains.

harvest to cut and bring in crops

hieratic simple form of hieroglyphs used for everyday writing and record keeping

hieroglyphics writing that uses pictures and symbols rather than letters to represent sounds or whole words. The word means 'sacred carving' in ancient Greek.

irrigation watering land by using man-made methods to bring the water to the fields

limestone grey or creamy-white rock that is fairly easy to work with

Lower Egypt area of Egypt from the Mediterranean shore to the city of Memphis

mummy body of a dead person that has been preserved, usually by embalming

obelisk pillar carved into a pyramid shape at the top

papyrus reed that grows in waterlogged land along the River Nile. The ancient Egyptians ate the young shoots of the plant. They pulled up the fully grown plants and used the stems to make boats. They used the inside pith to make paper.

pharaoh king who ruled ancient Egypt

preserve keep something in good condition

priest person who works in a temple serving a god or goddess

pyramid building made from stone with triangular sides that rise up from a square base and meet together at one point. They were used as tombs for important people.

sandstone rock made of sand, usually red, yellow, brown, grey, or white

scribe a person in ancient Egypt who could read and write. Scribes ran the country for the pharaoh and also acted as priests. They were the only people in ancient Egypt who could read and write.

shrine place where a statue of a god or goddess is kept where people can go to pray to the god or goddess

sphinx imaginary creature with the head of a woman and the winged body of a lion

Upper Egypt area from of Egypt from Memphis to the First Cataract

Valley of the Kings area in Egypt where many of the tombs of pharaohs from the New Kingdom have been found

widow woman whose husband has died

Index